It Begins With Me

It Begins With Me

SHAUNA SPELLMAN

StoryTerrace

Text Shauna Spellman
Copyright © Shauna Spellman

First print May 2023

StoryTerrace

www.StoryTerrace.com

CONTENTS

INTRODUCTION	9
WHO I CAME FROM	13
HOW IT WAS AT HOME	23
WHEN I WAS THREE	29
WHEN I WAS FOUR	33
WHEN I WAS FIVE	37
WHEN I WAS TEN	43
MY TEENS	47
THE HEALING BEGINS	55
THE "A" WORD	65
ALWAYS LEARNING	79
THERAPY	87
THE END OF MY FAMILY	99

WHERE I'M AT AND WHERE I'M GOING	119
WHAT I WANT YOU TO KNOW	125

INTRODUCTION

We are all products of those who made us and those who raised us, and to some extent, we will always be defined by our origins. But to what extent?
I believe that's up to us.

My parents were damaged people who raised two daughters very much the way they had been raised. They chose not to heal the wounds inflicted on them, and so they wounded my sister and me in our turn. The damage they did was not intentional. They loved me, and I loved them very much, despite the fact that their choices did me a great deal of harm. But they could have done otherwise. And did not.

When you are a child in a family that doesn't function well, you don't know any better, but as you get older, you can look back and understand who you came from, not from the perspective of the child you were, but with the maturity and wisdom of an adult who knows they have the capacity to grow and heal. It took me a long time to see that my parents were just damaged people who did as they'd been raised to do. I could have carried on in their footsteps. Instead, I chose to heal.

It's as simple as that. I chose to break the patterns of my family and to get well.

It was a long, difficult process, but it began with a choice and continued with the same choice being made over and over again.

IT BEGINS WITH ME

My origins defined me. They were my foundation, but I defined what was built on that foundation.

Professional portrait of me. My hair and makeup were professionally done for this photo. One of the few I have.

WHO I CAME FROM

My Mother's Side

My maternal grandmother grew up on a small dairy farm in Lawrenceburg, Indiana, the eldest child of an Irish mother and a German father. My great-grandparents, whom we called Big Mom and Pop, were both very hard workers, as were their children, who had to work on the farm as soon as they were old enough. Every day, they got up early to milk the cows and fill glass bottles with milk to be delivered to people's doorsteps. My grandmother—Maga—developed a very strong work ethic. They didn't have an easy life, but they all had a great love for the animals they raised on their farm. My grandmother passed that love for animals on to my mother, and to me.

My mother's family traced their roots to the Daughters of the American Revolution and were always involved in that organization. They were also very religious; their entire social life revolved around the church. Maga was raised a Lutheran, but when she married my Episcopalian grandfather—whom we called Paga—she converted.

Paga grew up in a very dysfunctional family. His attorney father was a brilliant man, but he was also an alcoholic, and when his wife died in childbirth, leaving him alone with three children, things fell apart. My great-grandfather squandered his money, and his children often went without. My grandfather, the eldest, once wore women's shoes to school, because he had no others. Despite this difficult childhood, he went on to graduate Phi Beta Kappa from the Naval Academy.

After my grandparents married, they crossed the border from Lawrenceburg to Cincinnati, Ohio, where they had three children, the eldest of which was my mother, Mollie. She was born in 1930.

The Great Depression had just begun, and there were few work opportunities. My grandfather thought about what the people needed, no matter what, and decided to open what we called the Shop: a hair salon for men, which was later expanded to include women on the other side of the building. My mother and her siblings used to help out, even by doing hair. They were never wealthy, but they always got by and always shared with others. During that decade, destitute people would wander by their house, and my grandmother would always make them a plate of food.

After they closed up the Shop, my grandfather went to work for the IRS for quite a few years so he would get a retirement pension from the government. He did well, but I think both of my grandparents carried that Depression-era mentality to the end of their days. They were so thrifty, even when they no longer needed to be. There was always that fear lurking.

My mother excelled at math and wanted to study it, but back then, women didn't do such things—in fact, most women didn't go to college—and my grandfather convinced her to get a degree in business, instead. I suspect my grandparents probably couldn't afford to have my mother go away to school, so they sent her to the University of Cincinnati.

My Father's Side

When my grandfather was sixteen, his mother died in childbirth, leaving five children to be raised by an alcoholic father who beat his children and did not provide properly for them.

Grampie finished school, spent a few years in the Navy, and went to college. He was working as a stockbroker when the market crashed in 1929. Things got bad, and he started drinking. He met and married my grandmother, and they had a daughter named Shirley. My father was born four years later. The two siblings were very close.

My grandmother was a wonderful pianist. She earned a degree at the Juilliard School of Music and became a professional musician, making records and playing at places like the Metropolitan Opera House and Carnegie Hall. Though she was not an alcoholic herself, other members of her family were.

My grandparents had a very dysfunctional marriage and divorced when my dad was 13. My dad remembered feeling very ashamed, because divorce wasn't as accepted then as it is now. Grampie wasn't a support to my dad, because of his drinking, but my great aunt and uncle were very well off and paid for him to go to a good boarding school, which is where he was when he learned that his sister had died.

My grandmother was a Christian Scientist who put more stock in laying on of hands and prayer than in doctors and medicine. By the time my grandmother called a doctor, it was too late. Twenty-one-year-old Shirley died of Bright's disease, which, caught early, was treatable at the time. My grandfather had remarried and lived an hour away. He hadn't known how sick his daughter was, or he would have insisted she get help.

My 17-year-old father was not allowed to cry at the funeral. His mother forbade it.

He never talked about his sister's death. I don't believe he ever got over it.

My grandmother remarried, but when that marriage fell apart, so did she. She was hospitalized in a psychiatric facility, where she remained for a few years. My dad had two step-brothers and felt his step-father favored them. He finished school and went into the Navy.

My grandmother married a third time and remained married to this husband until she died.

My Parents

My dad served three years at the end of the war on a minesweeper called the USS Spokane doing the treacherous work of clearing mines in the ocean. After being honorably discharged, he got a degree in geology, met my mother, and married her.

They immediately moved to California for the warmer climate, but ended up in Iraq, where my dad helped the

IT BEGINS WITH ME

Bedouins find water. My sister was born in Baghdad. After two years, my dad was offered a contract doing similar work in Saudi Arabia, but I think they were homesick. My dad got a job in the San Francisco Bay Area, and soon they were getting ready to have me.

There was just one problem: my mom had scoliosis and had never gotten the treatment she needed. She was scheduled to have her spine fused when she learned she was pregnant with me. They did want more children, just not right then. Still, there I was.

My dad was working in the mountains at the time, nowhere near a hospital. There had been problems with my sister's birth, so my mom went back to Cincinnati and stayed with her parents to have me. I was born by C section in January 1959.

***

My mom once showed me two pictures of men in their Navy uniforms. My dad and his dad. I couldn't tell them apart.

My dad started drinking and smoking when he entered the Navy. He was a funny, brilliant, damaged man who binge-drank on weekends and evenings and hit my sister and me like his father had hit him, and like my great-grandfather had hit his son, and so on, back through our family line. From what I've gathered, all the males on my father's side of the family were alcoholics. There isn't a single female alcoholic in the family.

IT BEGINS WITH ME

My father inherited a disease and then was taught to bottle up his pain and never let it out.

Because he didn't deal with his pain, he inflicted pain on us.

My grandfather Grampie, step grandmother Alice and me on the front porch of his oceanfront house, Noank, Connecticut.

My Dad and his mother Grandma Polly in a nursing home in Guilford Connecticut. Visited the summer of senior year at UCLA

My grandparents Maga and Paga on their 60th wedding anniversary. Mom's parents. Cincinnati, Ohio. Such a happy day!

*My maternal grandparents. Maga and Paga on their wedding day.
Lawrenceburg, Indiana*

HOW IT WAS AT HOME

When I think back to my childhood, I remember playing Kick the Can and Hide and Seek and Marco Polo with the kids in my neighborhood. My friends and I rode our bikes until the streetlights came on, and hung out at the mall and the beach.

One of my best memories is from the summer when I was nine, and we went back east to visit all my grandparents. We started on the coast of Connecticut, where Grampie and Grandma Polly had retired. Grampie had a little motorboat, which he named after my sister, and a little rowboat, which he named after me. I remember going fishing in the motorboat—Grampie, my dad, my sister, and I. We puttered around all day, visiting some of the small islands and dropping anchor to fish. They taught us to bait our hooks and how to put the line down. We caught a lot of fish and some eels. I remember them throwing the eels back in, because we thought they were gross. I remember how happy we all were that day. We all loved the ocean. It was like we all found peace there.

Another vivid memory is from a Saturday when I was seven. I ran into my parents' room and jumped on their bed, accidentally landing on my dad's leg. He beat me so furiously that my mother had to stop him. He was completely out of control, and he wasn't even drunk.

My dad was two people, Dr. Jekyll and Mr. Hyde. Dad #1 and Dad #2.

Dad #1 was the dad who woke us early on Mother's Day so we could make pancakes for our mom and taught me so patiently to sail. He was the dad the neighborhood kids invited to play baseball, because he was so hilarious and fun to be around. He was so very proud when we did well.

Dad #2 was the dad who lurked in the shadows of a man's pain and disease. He came out when he drank, which was frequently, but he could come out at any time.

He often hit my sister and me with an open hand, but usually he just yelled terrible things at us and sometimes threw things at the wall. When I was little, this was especially upsetting to me. I could not comprehend what was going on. I remember feeling very confused and wanting desperately to know why my daddy was being this way.

I adored my dad, and I feared him. I was closer to him than I was to my mother or my sister, and I longed to escape him. On good days, we laughed a lot. On bad days, I felt tremendous fear. In general, I felt anger towards both my parents, who I knew should be my protectors, but who were not. I was alone in this family. I had to learn to survive on my own, to be resilient.

When there's alcoholism in the home, it's not a child-centered home, it's an alcohol-centered home. My mom was attuned more to my father's needs than she was to ours. We all were. We all revolved around him, a wary, frightened constellation tied to him by love and by the secrets our family kept close. There was a constant tension in the air in my family, an uncertainty and insecurity, a loneliness, a watchfulness.

I think one of the reasons I read people so well is that I spent so much my childhood tuned in to my father and where he was at. It paid to gauge his mood and how much he'd had to drink. Never knowing when he would blow was terrifying, and I never felt like I had any control over what was going to happen, so I was always looking for the signs. I became hypervigilant. We all did. It was how we survived.

Even today, when things are going well, I find myself waiting for the other shoe to drop.

There's an absolutely unspoken rule in a family plagued by alcoholism: what happens in the home stays in the home. You don't even talk about it in the home. We would have these horrible scenes and then would move on like nothing happened. I would go to church, or school, or out with friends, and I would never say a word about it. I held it all inside.

Of course, people knew. Neighbors heard the yelling and shouting. Adults at church and school were especially kind to me. The connections I made with these people made life bearable.

Such connections came less easily to my sister. I was deeply affected by what went in on our home, but I suspect I got off easy compared to her. I don't know what events shaped her before I came along or before I could remember. I do know that there were certain events that shaped me. They damaged me, but they also led me down the path to healing and to being the person I am today.

My Dad holding me dressed in a clown costume for Halloween.

*My Mom in the front yard with me running around. Looking up to no good!
Ticonderoga Drive, San Mateo, California*

My sister Mickey and I on July 4th. Mom handmade the red, white, and blue outfits we were wearing. San Mateo, California

WHEN I WAS THREE

Some of my earliest memories are of visiting my mom in the hospital after her back surgery, which finally took place when I was three. I remember how thrilled I was to see her. I missed her so much. I didn't really understand what was going on, just that my mom wasn't home, and I desperately wanted her to be.

When she finally came home, she was bedridden for nine months and couldn't take care of me.

I remember getting angry and going to her bed and saying, "When are you going to get out of this bed? I want you to get up!" I was confused and afraid and angry. I just wanted her to be my normal, regular mom again.

Maga came to look after us. She did everything for my mother and for us. She washed my mom's hair and give her sponge baths. At the beginning, she had to feed her, because she couldn't sit up. She took care of the household. She took us to church every Sunday and even got the priest to come to the house on Sundays and give my mom communion.

My father went to work and came home and ate dinner and sat in front of the TV and drank.

This upset Maga enormously. She would call my grandfather and complain to him that she was doing everything, and Buzz (that was my dad's nickname) wasn't even grateful. My mom had to listen to all this and couldn't do anything about the situation, so on top of her great physical pain, she was upset throughout her recovery.

My dad didn't see the problem. His job was to bring home the bacon and fix things around the house. My mother was responsible for the rest, and if she couldn't do it, Maga could. This was partly generational, and partly because he was often very selfish.

All this pain and confusion influenced me. So did my grandmother's loving, selfless act of caring for us despite my father making it even more challenging than it had to be. I became very close to Maga during this time.

When my mother was finally up and about, Maga went back to Cincinnati, and my parents made the decision to move to Southern California for the climate.

Me holding my favorite dolly Thumbelina. I was three years old in San Mateo, California.

WHEN I WAS FOUR

One thing everyone in my family had in common was a love of animals. Even my dad had a soft spot for those sweet members of our family.

The very first dog I ever had was Mickey, a Shetland sheepdog. We got him when I was one or two, and both my sister and I were completely crazy about him. I used to sit on our back steps and put my arm around him and "read" my favorite book to him. My parents and sister were always busy with something, but Mickey was there giving me unconditional love.

When I was four, Mickey got sick and had to be put down. I was absolutely devastated, but his death hit my mom particularly hard.

I don't think Mickey's death was the reason for what happened next, but perhaps it contributed. At around this time, my mom began to cry and couldn't seem to stop. She cried and cried and cried. I would find her on her knees and think she was trying to pray. Then she would put her head in her hands and lean on the bed and sob.

My dad didn't seem to know what to do. He would get up, get my sister off to school, and get himself to work, and I was left alone with my crying mother.

I was so confused and scared and alone. I would say, over and over, "Mommy, Mommy, why are you crying? What can I do?"

Even I knew it wasn't really about Mickey's death. Something else was going on, something I could sense, but I was too young to understand the physical pain she was going through from her surgery. I was too young to understand that the wounds of her childhood had never been healed, and that they were still hurting her, and on top of all that, she had to deal with the burdens that my father's alcoholism placed on her, and all of us. All I knew was that my mother was crying, and I wanted her to stop.

I begged her to stop crying, the way I had begged her to get out of bed when she was recovering from her surgery, but her nervous breakdown, as we later called it, lasted for weeks. To my little four-year-old self, it felt like forever.

And then one day, the crying stopped, and she started functioning again. My parents found a house in Temple City, and we settled there for the next five years.

Even after my mom got better, she refused to get another dog, despite my persistent begging for one. Every time I asked, she would tell me that she couldn't go through that again.

One day I said to her, "Mom, life is for the living. Mickey died. That doesn't mean we can't get another dog."

So, after four years of me driving them crazy, we got a miniature Dachshund named Fritzie, and from then on, we had dogs and other animals. When they died, we had a little ceremony in the backyard, where we would bury their ashes. I credit those animals with giving me something I really needed to get through those times.

***

Years later, a therapist would say that my mother's surgery and her breakdown were two pivotal points in my development, largely because they happened at such an early age. The lesson I learned from these events was threefold: 1. No one was taking care of me. 2. I needed to take care of others. 3. I had to take care of myself.

My sister and I playing in the sandbox in our backyard at our new home on Olive Street. Temple City, California

WHEN I WAS FIVE

A lot of kids have separation anxiety when they start school. They cry, and they cling, and they just want to be home.

I was elated. I looked forward to every day of school. I loved my Kindergarten teacher. I made fun friends. I was free from all the turmoil at home. I was safe.

I didn't know it at the time, but my great escape had been delayed by my mother. Whenever I asked my mom when I could go to preschool like my sister had, she would tell me I had to wait until I was five. When I was older, she admitted that it had been selfish of her to keep me at home, but she said she wasn't ready to let me go yet. After her surgery, the orthopedic surgeon explained that her back wouldn't be strong enough for her to carry a child to term. She was holding on to her last baby as long as she could.

She later said to me, "Shauna, that's when I realized that God knew so much better than me."

I loved school all the way through and did well both academically and socially. I learned to get involved as a way of escaping my home life. I joined the swim team, I took up dance, and played in the band. When I got older, I added on activities outside school. I was a Candy Striper and a Girl Scout, and I hung out as much as I could with friends. I was happy when I was out doing these things. When I was at home or with my family I was often sad and lonely.

Not all my friends were kids.

The house in Temple City was on a very small cul-de-sac with six tiny houses set close together. Sylvia and Jack and their teenage son Rob lived across from us and two doors up on the street. I don't remember how this came about, but shortly after we moved in, I started going to Sylvia's house to play. I remember always being so thrilled when I could go to Sylvia's. The only time she ever turned me away was if she had a migraine.

I wasn't close to Jack or Rob, but they were kind to me. I remember sharing a lot of their life. I think I went to Sylvia looking for the things I wasn't getting at home, like a sense of security and consistency and warmth. She was always so kind and happy to see me. I felt safe with her and close to her. Fortunately, my parents seemed to value my friendship with this adult woman.

When I was eight or nine, Rob was drafted to go to Vietnam. Jack and Sylvia were both extremely upset. There were a lot of days during Rob's tour of duty when Sylvia wasn't up for visits from me. I would go home and tell my parents that Sylvia was too worried about Rob to play with me, and they would lead us in a prayer for Rob and his parents.

Not long after Rob came home from Vietnam (in one piece!), my parents decided it was time to move. We were doing better financially. They wanted a bigger house with a pool. They found one in upper Arcadia, an upper middle class area of the city.

I remember being very sad when we moved. Sylvia wasn't going to be two houses away from me anymore.

Sylvia wanted to see where we had moved, so my mom invited her to the new house. We showed her around and had lunch. Sylvia gave me a little stuffed bunny.

We stayed in touch for a while. We even went to Rob's wedding the next summer—the first wedding I ever went to—but in time, we drifted apart. I was busy with school and friends and the things kids do. I suppose in some ways, I had outgrown the friendship of a grown woman who played paper dolls with me and gave me a safe space. Perhaps if we hadn't been so far apart physically, things would have been different. Things were getting worse at home. Perhaps she would have continued to provide solid footing for me, to be one of my angels.

***

Not long ago, I found that stuffed bunny in my storage, all torn up and looking its age. At first, it was a stranger to me. It had sat all those years in my parents' house and then in my storage. Why had I kept it? Then I remembered Sylvia giving it to me. I remembered Sylvia.

This friendship with an adult woman gave me so much. I would later connect with teachers and a Sunday School teacher. Much later, when I was in therapy, I remember feeling ashamed that I had sought out affection and connection with these people, and being told that this was a healthy thing, that I should honor the part of myself that reached out to ask for what was lacking. This was something no one else in my family ever did. The fact that I had it in me to do this defined the path that my life took.

Kindergarten

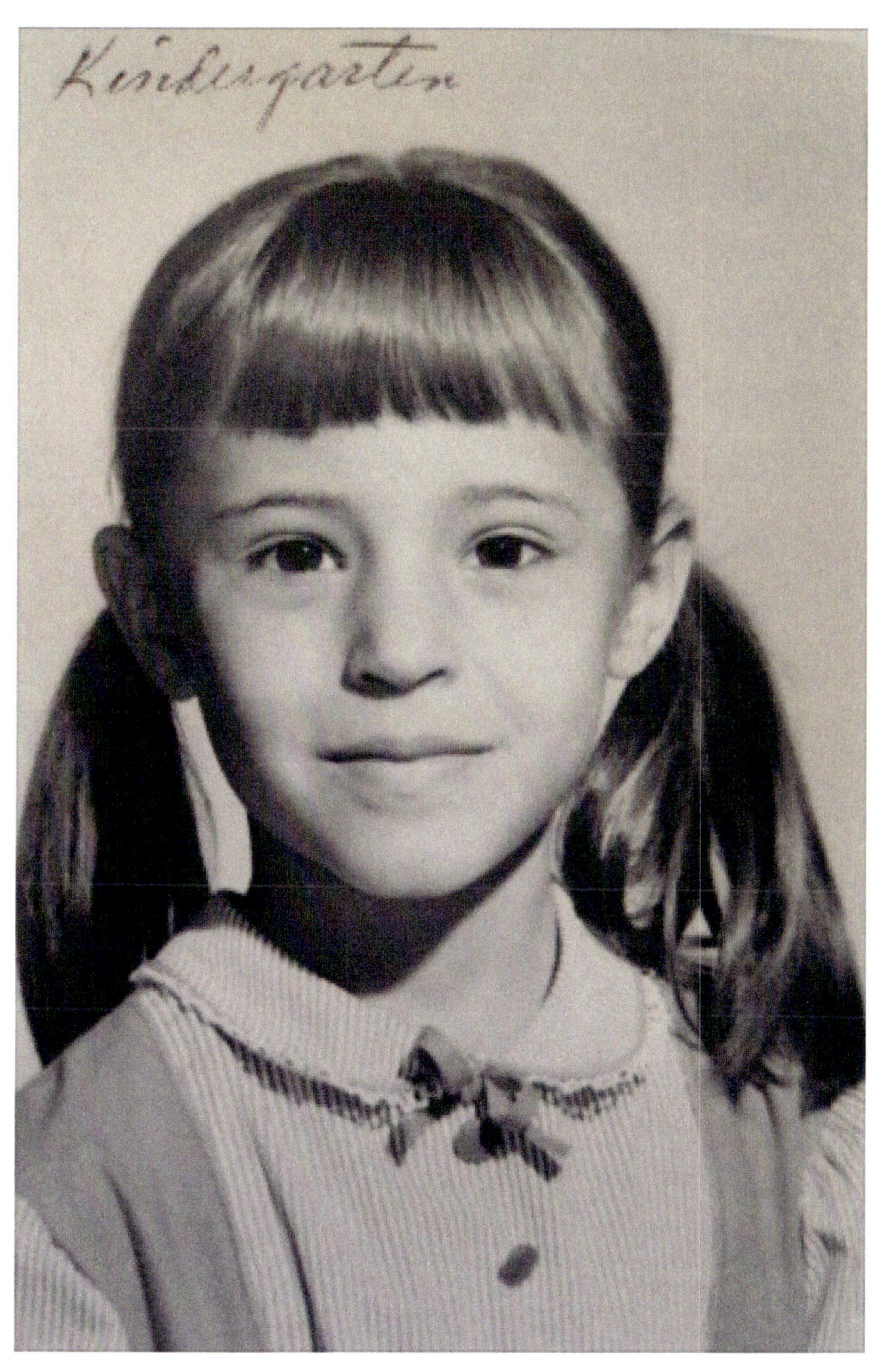

My kindergarten school photo. I was 5 years old. Longley Way Elementary School Arcadia California Love those pigtails!

WHEN I WAS TEN

One summer day, shortly after we'd moved into our new house in Arcadia, I learned what never to do with my dad.

My sister was away at Girl Scout camp, and my mom went for tea at a neighbor's, and I was left at home alone with my dad.

That day, he had started drinking in the morning, one beer after another. He went into the backyard and threw up and then came in and drank some more. I was 10. I was starting to understand that when he drank like that, bad things happened, so at one point when he went to get another beer, I ran up and tried to grab it from him and begged him not to drink anymore.

He glared at me and said, "Don't you ever do that again, Shauna. Don't you ever tell me not to drink." He was terrifyingly angry. I got out of there fast.

I decided to go for a swim. My dad came out and got in the pool too, and he seemed OK. We were horsing around when all of a sudden, he grabbed me and shoved me under the water and held me there. When I started struggling, he finally let me up for air. And then he did it again. And again. I honestly don't remember how many times, because it was so upsetting and so terrifying for me. Every time I came up, I yelled, "Please Daddy, please stop! Please don't!"

He did eventually stop. I got out of the pool and ran into the house and stayed away from him for the rest of the day. Eventually my mother came home, and I told her what had happened and that I had been scared to death. She was very, very upset.

That evening, he seemed better, so I watched TV with him. He sat on the couch peeling a peach with a small knife while I sat on a nearby chair.

All of a sudden, he said to the peach, "I'm gonna stab you. That's right. I'm going to stick this knife into you." He was looking at the peach, but I knew the words were meant for me.

I sat there, frozen with fear. I didn't know what to do. When he didn't say or do anything else, I got up and went to tell my mother. She comforted me. She didn't say anything to him. He was still drunk. There was nothing she could say to him at that point.

That night, I lay in bed shivering. It wasn't cold in my room, but my whole body shook. My teeth chattered. I was afraid to go to sleep.

I don't know if my dad remembered what he had done, or if he had a blackout. I do know that we never talked about it. And I never could forget it.

***

When I tell this story in Al Anon, everyone gasps. They all know you don't get between an alcoholic and their alcohol.

IT BEGINS WITH ME

In those days, I didn't even know my dad was an alcoholic, but I learned my lesson well. I never tried to stop him from drinking again.

My fifth-grade school photo. Highland Oaks Elementary School in Arcadia California I was 10 years old had braces then.

MY TEENS

When I was little, I didn't know my family wasn't healthy—I had nothing to compare it to—but when I got into my teens, I would go over to other people's houses and see that their parents didn't drink like my dad did. There wasn't a tension in the air. I began to realize something was wrong. I began to want my family to be more like these other families.

My dad was always angry about something. We were always in trouble for some reason. While his drinking got worse, the violence actually decreased. We got big enough to fight back, and we did. But now I found myself embarrassed by my dad's behavior. There were times when I just wanted to crawl in a hole and hide.

One time, I had my friends over for a swim. It was nighttime, and we had decided to skinny dip. We were laughing and horsing around when my dad came out and turned on the floodlights. They lit up the pool like they were the sun. He yelled and screamed at all of us as we swam to the side of the pool to hide our nakedness. I was absolutely mortified. Eventually he went back in the house. We got out and put our bathing suits back on and wrapped ourselves up in towels. We had been having so much fun, and just like that, it was ruined.

Another time, we were vacationing in Orange County, Newport Beach. It was my mom's vacation too, so my dad always took us out for dinner so she didn't have to cook. He would also let us invite a friend along if we liked. That was one of the nice things about him. He could be generous.

One night, we were waiting for a table at a crowded restaurant. Dad was drinking. There was a muscular man sitting at the bar, and we were calling him Mr. Atlas because of his muscles. My dad jumped up and yelled out, "Atlas, party of one!" Loudly. Everyone looked. We giggled a bit—we were teens—but we were so embarrassed.

There were many of these embarrassing, awkward moments in front of friends and in public places. I was powerless to do anything about them. All I could do was plan for the future. From eighth grade on, my focus was on doing well academically so I could get accepted into a good school where I could live in the dorms, far from my family, and get a good education.

One bright spot during those years was the friendships I formed with three girls from school. I didn't trust easily, but I seemed to know who to trust. We talked about classes, people we liked (and people we didn't), politics, stuff going on in school, and teachers. We rode our bikes to the department store. We did goofy things and got into trouble. We had so much fun.

We also had so much in common. We were all the children of an alcoholic and never talked about it. We complained about the things girls complain about to their friends, but we didn't talk about beatings, or a parent throwing things, or them being incoherent, or us being terrified of them. We didn't talk about how we never felt safe, how we were always afraid, how we lived our lives waiting for the other shoe to drop. We left the alcohol and the damage it was doing out of the picture. We created an oasis of friendship together.

Years later, when I wondered aloud to a therapist about these girls and this friendship we shared, she said that we had been attracted to each other because we felt a familiarity. There was something about how we all moved and operated in the world that we recognized, because we moved the same way. We were part of a club, and in that club, we gave each other what we all needed: An escape. A crew. Companionship. Fun. At home, we struggled and suffered. When we were together, we could be kids. We were safe in each other's care. I am still friends with all of them today.

Unfortunately, this was something my sister lacked. She didn't make friends easily. I believe that this played a role in what happened later.

My family did have good times during those years, particularly when we took vacations at Newport Beach, but the tension in the air wore on me. I didn't want to always be walking on eggshells. I wanted to be free.

And eventually, I was. I graduated from high school and got in to UCLA.

My lifelong friend Lisa. We met at age 10 at Highland Oaks Elementary School, Arcadia California. Senior yearbook photo

Mat Maidens. Front Row: Tracey Johnson, Rhonda Golling, Shawna Spellman. Back Row: Sharon Anderson, Nancy Coleman, Margie Accardo, Julie Francis, Patty Malden.

Junior year at Arcadia High School. My history teacher, the wrestling coach, asked me to be a Mat Maiden for the team.

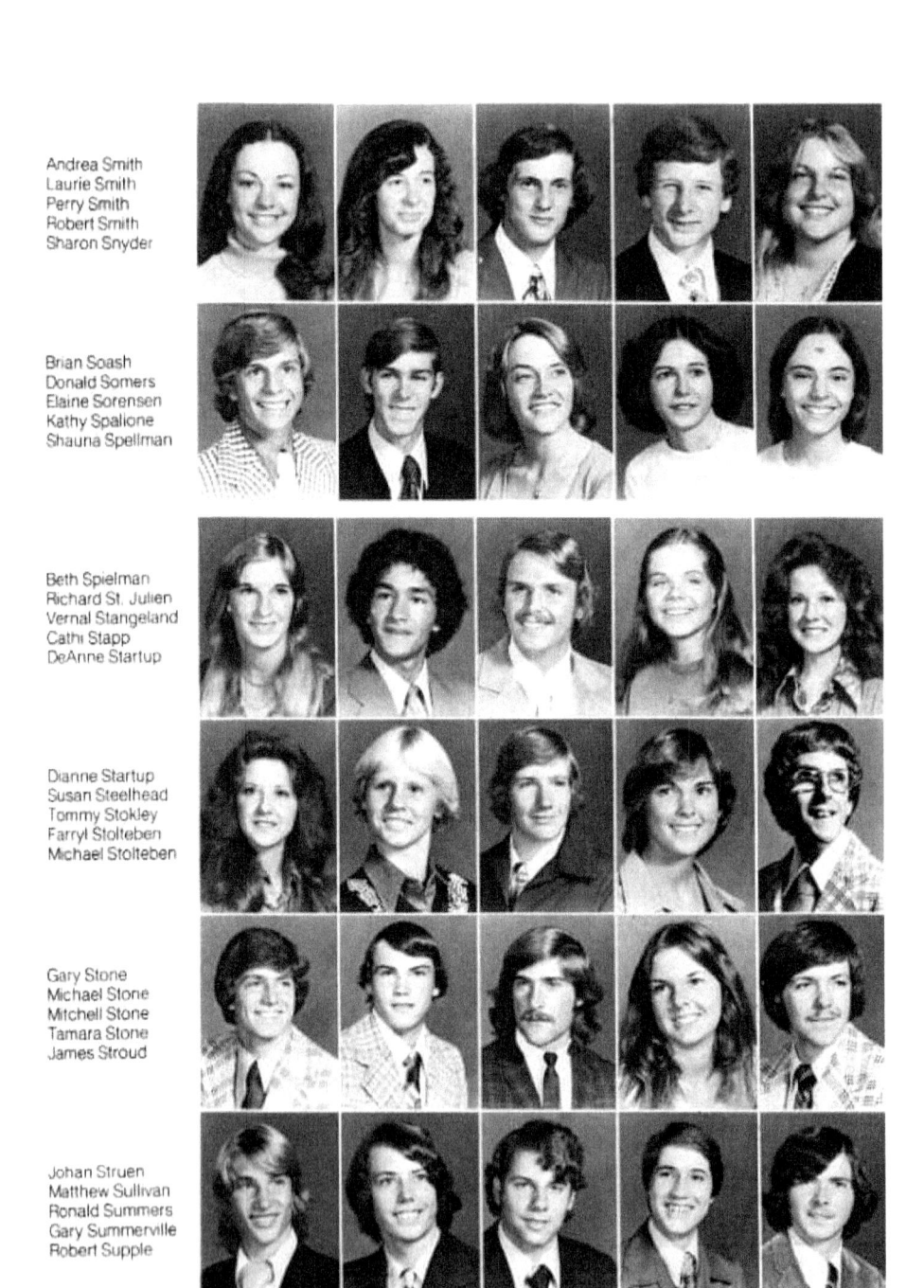

Andrea Smith
Laurie Smith
Perry Smith
Robert Smith
Sharon Snyder

Brian Soash
Donald Somers
Elaine Sorensen
Kathy Spalione
Shauna Spellman

Beth Spielman
Richard St. Julien
Vernal Stangeland
Cathi Stapp
DeAnne Startup

Dianne Startup
Susan Steelhead
Tommy Stokley
Farryl Stolteben
Michael Stolteben

Gary Stone
Michael Stone
Mitchell Stone
Tamara Stone
James Stroud

Johan Struen
Matthew Sullivan
Ronald Summers
Gary Summerville
Robert Supple

My Arcadia High School Senior Portrait for the yearbook, 1977.

My lifelong friend Sue. We met at age 12 at Foothills Junior High School Arcadia, California. Senior yearbook photo.

THE HEALING BEGINS

Starting UCLA was an echo of starting Kindergarten. While other students were desperately homesick and counted the days until the weekend when they could see their families, I reveled in my distance from home. Throughout primary and high school, I had been safe and free in the day. Now I was safe and free all the time. I didn't have to see my family at all if I didn't want to. When I did, I could walk away when things got ugly. I didn't have to deal with any of that anymore. Ever.

Except that I did. Just not in the way I imagined.

My life had improved on the surface, but underneath, the pressure was building. I was depressed, and I couldn't seem to pull myself out of it. I began to realize that being away from my family wasn't enough. I needed help. When my roommate, Gloria, told me that I could get free counseling at the Student Health Center, I was blown away. I had no idea.

I had asked to see a counselor when I was 13, and my parents took my sister to see one because she was acting out, but they said they couldn't afford it and that I didn't need it. My sister was the sick one. Not me. I now know that label is called the identified patient. The one person in the family who gets labeled as "sick" when really the entire family system is sick. Now help was available for free. I took it.

To this day, I get emotional when I talk about the therapist I worked with for the next three years.

IT BEGINS WITH ME

Julie practiced psycho-dynamic therapy, which focuses on the relationship between client and therapist. She got me on medication for anxiety and depression, and we worked on how things that were happening in my life in the present impacted me. She told me that I had swallowed so much guilt and anger and sadness and grief for so many years that it had filled me up. I needed to let it out. She would help me understand what had happened and help me find better ways to function.

About a year in to therapy, I was rejected by a guy. The rejection hit me hard. I started crying and couldn't stop. Julie helped me to understand that I wasn't crying because the guy rejected me; it was just the straw that broke the camel's back. I was finally in a place where I could cry about the rejection I had experienced in my family. I was in a safe place where someone was helping me. The dam had broken and let it all out. There was no stopping it now!

I wasn't allowed to cry in my family. Not really. If I did, they'd get angry and tell me to stop or that they'd give me something to cry about. I learned to hold everything inside, just as my parents had learned to hold everything inside when they were young. When I was four, my mom had found she couldn't bottle it up anymore, and she cried. The difference was that she bottled it up again. I wasn't going to do that. I was going to move forward, with Julie's help.

When I was at my worst, I would tell Julie that I had barely gotten out of bed, gotten dressed, gotten to my session, and she would say, "But you did. You're doing it, Shauna. It won't last forever. You'll come out the other end."

IT BEGINS WITH ME

And when I did come out the other end, she told me, "Shauna, for the first time in your life, you were able to work with depression all the way through. You were able to finally release and let all of that out."

My dad had released everything with alcohol. When my mother's dam broke, she plugged the holes in it and carried on. My sister had acted out and closed herself off from other people. I was doing something they had not done.

Julie did something no one in my family had ever done. She was there for me at all times. She gave me her home number in case I ever needed her and her boyfriend's number in San Francisco for when she visited him on weekends. I never did call those numbers, but that gesture did me so much good. It was so powerful. She really, truly cared, and she did so in such a positive way. I had a boyfriend at one point who could always tell when I'd just seen Julie, because I was lighter and happier. In part, this was because she was such a support to me, but also because she always ended our sessions on an upbeat note. I didn't realize it at the time, but she was giving me hope.

When my parents found out I was getting therapy, they were both really upset. I think they were worried about what I was telling Julie, because they knew that a lot of what went on during my childhood was inappropriate. Julie told me that the first instinct when someone in the family system pulls out and starts to get better is for the other family members to try to pull them back down. She said this reaction was evidence of my healing.

IT BEGINS WITH ME

As I started to feel better about myself, I interacted differently with my family. Behavior that I had to tolerate as a child, I no longer tolerated. My mom told me that my dad was behaving better because he wanted me to come around more. My dad told me that I had changed, and he meant it in a good way. Things got better with them, though we never had the sort of relationship other people have with their parents. It was always strained. There was always pain.

But the pain had lessened. I had learned how to let it out, and so much more. I had started developing self-esteem and self-worth and confidence. I was speaking up for myself, asserting myself. I was healing.

In my third year, Julie told me that she had finished her degree and wouldn't be staying in the LA area. She had tears in her eyes when she told me this. She said that there were two people she was feeling particularly bad about leaving: me and a twelve-year-old girl she had been working with.

I went back to my sorority house and sat and cried. It did help that she had gotten emotional when she told me she was leaving me. I knew she truly cared, that the connection went both ways. But I grieved the loss of her for a long time. Even today, Julie is one of the most important people in my life. She is the person I first talked to about my family. She was always, always on my side. She helped me understand what had happened to me in my family and that I could heal. She set me on the path to healing, and gave me hope that things would get better. For that, I will always be grateful.

I knew Julie was special. I didn't realize just how special until I had others to compare her to—therapists I saw after her, and then ones I worked with when I got into the field myself.

***

Julie focused on me. Ruth, the therapist she recommended, stepped back to look at our family. This was a real eye-opener for me.

To my surprise, my parents agreed to come to a single family session, which Ruth and another therapist observed. Then Ruth and I talked on our own.

Ruth said there was a lot of stuff going on in that session, but that she sensed love in the room. She said we all sat apart from each other and that my mom had gone to the back corner of the room, almost like she was hiding herself. Both therapists could see how low her self-esteem was. She said neither my father or sister were acting normal. She said they acted like they were "bombed," meaning drunk. Neither one had been drinking. They had stared vacantly, unable to engage. She said that other people would have noticed it, but to me it was normal. I couldn't see what an outsider could.

She also told me that I was by far the healthiest person in my family and that she was going to help me to become even more healthy. And she did.

She also helped me to see my family more clearly. One day, I was going on about how angry I was with them, how horrible they were, and she stopped me.

"Shauna," she said, "obviously they did some things right. Look at the person you turned out to be."

I stared at her. I had never thought about that. I only thought about what they did wrong.

Then she said, "The opposite of love is not hate. It's indifference, and you are far from indifferent about your parents."

That blew me away. She was right. I wasn't indifferent. I was just deeply hurt and angry, but I loved my parents very, very much. And they weren't indifferent either. They came to that session even though they really didn't want to.

***

I had a few therapists after Ruth. One of them encouraged me to use the word "functional" to describe my family, instead of "normal." Normal is what we're used to. My family was normal to me, but it wasn't functional. It didn't work.

All of my therapists said the same thing to me about how I had embraced healing. They said it took a lot of emotional strength and a lot of courage to reach out for help and that I did it at such a young age and that they admired that in me. They said that my willingness to look at painful things and work through difficult things was amazing. I kept coming back. I kept working to heal.

I stopped therapy after I graduated. I'd had some good therapists, but none I'd connected with as I had with Julie. Also, it was costing me money now. And I was doing better.

I wish I could say there was a happy ending, that my family got well and became functional. It never did. But I did.

My junior year Chi Omega Sorority party. With my date I knew from a job we worked together. Mexican theme. So much fun!

Senior year at UCLA, with my boyfriend Phil. We were out to dinner at an oceanfront restaurant, The Shanty, in Malibu

My dorm roommate Gloria, another dorm friend Karen me rafting on the Truckee River Lake Tahoe. Truckin' on the Truckee.

Maga, cousins Joni, Jon, and me. A day at King's Island Amusement Park, Cincinnati, Ohio

THE "A" WORD

After earning my bachelor's degree, I got a job in the Veterans Administration in West Los Angeles working on the psychiatric side of the facility. I had an interest because there are lot of veterans in my family. I had studied to work in this field, and found myself learning more on the job.

But I wasn't only learning about the job. During my second year there, a woman named Angela transferred onto my unit, and we became friendly, hanging out during and after work. One day, we were talking about one of the veterans who had a problem with alcohol, as many of them did, and I found myself telling her about my dad and his drinking. I described an episode that took place on the 4th of July, 1976, when I was 17.

That year was the bicentennial of the United States, and it was a really big deal. There were all sorts of events happening that went beyond the usual 4th of July festivities. It was a time for celebration.

But not in my home. For days, I had been able to feel the tension building in my dad, and therefore in all of us. I found myself trying to figure out how he was doing. At that point in my life, I had become very intuitive about my dad's emotional state. I could tell when he was getting ready to blow, which meant it was best to stay away.

He was getting ready to blow.

Fortunately, I had plans to go to Newport Beach with several girlfriends from high school. There were good waves that day. We hung out and body-surfed and flirted with surfers. We went for lunch down where they have the Balboa Fun Zone and the Newport Pier. We had such a blast.

There were going to be fireworks that evening, so I went home to get changed. I was just in time to witness my dad losing it.

I wasn't surprised by this, but I was shocked at the intensity of this particular blowout. Sometimes when he was angry, he would yell and throw something at the wall. This time, he had been drinking all day, and he was completely out of control, yelling and screaming and not making a lot of sense. Then he started throwing furniture and other things from the house into the yard and in the pool. It was the worst I had ever seen him.

It was very disturbing to see him just go crazy like that. I was very, very frightened, as were my mother and sister. My mother called a family friend and explained what was going on. We left my dad raging and throwing things and went to stay at the friend's home in South Arcadia.

And that was the end of my bicentennial 4th of July celebrations. Fireworks in my home instead of in the sky. That's how I described it to Angela.

The next morning, we were all afraid to go back to the house, but we went, anyway.

The place was in shambles. My dad was a shambles too, but he was calm and repentant, as he always was after a blow out. He was also still drunk. We later learned that the police had come after we left. One of the neighbors must have called.

My dad came to me later and told me that the reason he'd blown was that he was upset with my mom. I remember I felt some relief when he told me that it wasn't me. I'm not sure if he did that because he felt guilty that he'd upset us. I'm not sure he even knew what had made him lose it. Years later, I learned that he went to each of us individually and told us the same thing: he wasn't upset with us. He told my sister he was upset with our mom. He told our mom he was upset with us.

A few days after the episode, he called a family meeting. I remember sitting down at the kitchen table and thinking, *Oh my God, what is he going to say?*

But he surprised me. He said he'd behaved that way because of his drinking. He promised to never touch another drop.

We all just sat there and looked at him. We talked a little about what had happened. Mostly we just sat and listened. I was too scared to say much. Then we all got up and went on with our day. I think none of us really believed him, which is a good thing, because in no time, he was drinking again.

Years later, when I embarked on a 12 Step Program, I would learn that what he did that day was typical of alcoholics. The remorse, the repentance, the promise to stop, and then the breaking of the promise. At that point, though, I wasn't using the 'A' word to describe my dad.

I was used to my dad's drinking and his temper, but this incident hit me hard. When my mom's parents found out about it, they offered to fly me and my sister to Cincinnati to stay with them for the rest of the summer. I jumped at the offer. I wanted to be as far from my home as possible, and I sure didn't want to go on summer vacation with my parents, as we usually did in August.

At the end of July, I finished summer school and flew east, away from my dad.

My grandparents were such angels. They had noticed what a nervous wreck I was when we arrived, and they were concerned about both me and my sister. They took us out, and we did all sorts of fun things together. My aunt and uncle and cousins embraced us, telling us they were sorry for what had happened, but so glad that we had come, that they were so glad to see us. That all helped.

I went home at the end of August feeling somewhat restored, but also determined. I would finish my last year of high school, and then I'd leave home for good.

This is the story I told to Angela that day, a decade after the fact.

Angela listened attentively throughout. Then she said, "Well, Shauna, it sounds like he's an alcoholic."

I remember I just stared at her in shock. Then I said, "Well, I've always thought my dad was a problem-drinker. He doesn't handle his alcohol well, but an alcoholic?"

It sounds crazy, but despite the fact that I had done quite a bit of therapy at that point, the word "alcoholic" had never been mentioned. My therapists and I would talk about the fact that my dad drank, but I guess that because the focus of psycho-dynamic therapy is the relationship between the therapist and client, on how I was affected, we didn't talk that much about my family. They also didn't use a lot of terminology. They had to realize he was an alcoholic—there's no way they didn't—but they never used the word. Nor had I. Not even to myself.

Angela said, "Well, it sounds like it's more than that, Shauna. He really sounds like an alcoholic."

I just sat there processing her words. The idea didn't want to go into my head. I was 27. I had lived in this family my entire life. How could this be the first time I was hearing this word in relation to my dad? But deep down, I knew she was right. My dad was a full-blown alcoholic. He had the disease.

Armed with this word, with this truth that had not been spoken before in regards to my father, I began to review my life through a new lens. I thought about my three closest school friends who all had an alcoholic parent and had never spoken the word "alcoholic" to me either. We never went there. We never said the word. We didn't even think it. But I had known, just as they had known. It had been taboo to speak of my dad's drinking to others. It had been a secret within the family, something to be hidden, just as it had been in the homes of those three friends.

But now the word had been said aloud. My dad's disease had been named. There was no going back, at least not for me.

Al Anon

What Angela had said dropped a seed in the path of my life. Another seed came a few years later when I read an article about the effect of one person's alcoholism on the rest of the family. My dad's drinking had affected me and my sister and my mother. It had contributed to the people we became. I was beginning to think in a new way about my dad's drinking and my family and myself.

A few more years went by. I sometimes fell into a depression, especially after I was laid off from my job in the early 1990s. We were in a recession, and I couldn't find work in my field. I was so discouraged, because my identity has always been wrapped up in my work or school. When I wasn't achieving, I didn't feel valuable. I felt like I was falling apart again.

To make ends meet, I got work here and there as a movie extra and as a waitress at high-end catered events. At one event, a fellow waiter started talking about his father being an alcoholic, and how he went to these meetings and how they helped him deal with it. It had never crossed my mind that people would go to meetings and talk about such a thing.

Another seed was planted one day when I was doing extra work. I was chatting with a woman on the set, and somehow we got to talking about the fact that somebody in her family was an alcoholic and how she went to these meetings where she talked about how much they helped her. This woman actually gave me a program with dates and times and locations of meetings.

IT BEGINS WITH ME

I hung on to the program, and not long after this, I was on the Catalina Express to Catalina Island with a friend, and I met a woman who told me her life story. She'd had an alcoholic parent. She'd been married and divorced twice, both times to alcoholics. She had begun drinking heavily herself when she found out about Al Anon. Attending Al Anon meetings made her feel better. She had divorced her alcoholic husband and married the man she was sitting with on the ferry that day. Whereas her alcoholic husbands had treated her badly, this man treated her well. She told me that she didn't think she'd still be here if it weren't for Al Anon.

At that time, I was dating an alcoholic who treated me badly. I remember how her story felt so powerful to me, and the swirl of thoughts in my head. I thought of the other alcoholics I had dated and my friends asking me why I dated these guys when there were nice guys out there, guys would would treat me well.

That meeting on the Catalina Express was the seed that led me to my first Al Anon meeting on October 6th, 1992. I was feeling so bad that Wednesday, and I was desperate for help. I didn't have a therapist or a roommate to talk to. I was alone. But I had that program from the movie extra, and those strangers' words about how these meetings had helped them. I found a meeting at a church near where I lived. I still remember walking into the church, not knowing what to expect. My heart was pounding, but I was so desperate that I went in anyway. I sat in a chair in the circle, and people were so welcoming, or I might have turned around and fled. Instead, I sat and listened, and I was blown away.

These people were telling my story.

After the meeting, people came up to say hi and to invite me back. I went back the next week, and again, I listened, but the following week, I got my nerve up and raised my hand, and for the first time in my life, I shared.

That's what 12 Step programs call it—sharing. Sharing your experience, your strength, and your hope. Sharing is what the meetings are.

I talked about why I was there, and these people sat and listened to me. No one interrupted or commented. They just listened, respectfully and with interest. It was one of the most powerful experiences of my life. I didn't need to explain to anyone in the room what my dad was like, what my family was like. Everybody in the room loved an alcoholic. I'd tell them something my dad did, and they would tell me something their child or partner did, and it was the same. We were all from different backgrounds, races, belief systems, all had a different story, but we were also all the same. I felt that the trail of seeds brought me home, but to a healthier home than I had ever known before, a home where I was heard and understood and helped to heal. I felt such an enormous relief.

I kept attending that meeting and got to know some people. Someone suggested other meetings that they thought might be good for me if I felt I needed them. All meetings are different. I started going to more than one meeting, and I started meeting people and making friends at some of them. This is called fellowship in the 12 Step programs. I really started to get into that.

IT BEGINS WITH ME

I also started learning about the disease, about what it does to the person and to those close to them. I learned that the alcoholic gets sicker over time, and the family gets sicker with them. I looked at my family and saw the truth of that. We were all getting worse. New wounds were made on old wounds, and nothing got healed. The anger and the guilt, the pain and the shame, were all bottled up. I had begun to let them out while in therapy at UCLA, but I saw now that I needed an outlet. Sharing at meetings was my outlet.

They say recovery is like peeling away layers of the onion. There were a lot of ah-ha! moments and then all the bridges forming between them, deepening my understanding of alcoholism and inter-generational trauma. I began to see why my father was the way he was and to communicate better with him, and with my mother and sister. Some of my anger towards him ebbed. I saw that my family wasn't trying to destroy me. They just didn't know how to deal with their own problems.

I realized that I had been walking around in a fog my entire life. Now, many things became crystal clear to me. I looked back at old relationships. I saw that just as there had been an unconscious pull between me and my friends with alcoholic parents when I was a girl, I was attracted to the familiar in the men I dated. Over the years, almost all the men I had dated had either had an alcoholic parent or been an alcoholic themselves. The problem was that while my friendships were helpful, just as my new connections with people who had been damaged by alcoholism were helpful, my relationships with these men were not. My friends and the people at Al Anon

IT BEGINS WITH ME

were making our shared connection work for us. We were learning from each other, supporting each other. I couldn't choose my family, but I could choose my friends and the guys I dated. Those were choices. My choices.

I also learned that those people who had dropped seeds for me that led me to the Al Anon Family were the service step in the 12 Step program. They were carrying the message to others. I've carried the message to others the way those three people carried it to me so that I could receive it when I was ready. This book is another way for me to carry the message to those who still suffer.

***

A few years after I started going to meetings, I was attending one in the basement of a church and realized it was an Episcopal Church. I had stopped going to church when I left home. After the meeting, I went upstairs to check the service time.

I attended a service. That was 30 years ago. To this day, I am an active member of the Episcopal Church.

A photographer friend took some photos of me outside. This is one of the best ones.

My sister, her husband and my nephew had a professional family portrait. Good photo of all of them together.

Mr. Mistoffeles (Misty) Cassandra Named for characters in the play Cats I had just seen My first two cats littermates.

ALWAYS LEARNING

Shortly after I started with Al Anon, I began thinking seriously about making career changes. I wanted to get away from working inpatient with adults with psychiatric problems, but also from the sorts of workplaces I'd been in. I had moved from job to job, because they didn't pay well, and the management often didn't treat employees well, but there was also something very lacking in how these places treated the patients who were there to get help.

There were of course people who cared and gave a great deal, but they were in the minority. Many of them lacked empathy and self-awareness and their own mental health. In California, we were given ten hours towards our license for every hour in personal therapy. Perhaps 5-10% of the people I worked with took advantage of this. These people would never go above and beyond. If a person ran out of insurance, they'd be immediately discharged. There was no effort made to work out a payment arrangement or work on a sliding scale. I was disappointed and disheartened by what I saw. Vulnerable people were being taken advantage of. Even the staff were being used so someone could make money. There were so many professions an uncaring person could do well in, and they picked this one? It seemed criminal to me that these people would present themselves as helpers to those who desperately needed help, and then provide it in such a half-hearted, lackluster way. They lacked professionalism and integrity. They were obviously doing it for the money.

Ironically, it was a nudge from my dad that got me to make a change. My dad had his problems, but he had a great deal of integrity. He sat me down one day and told me that he was concerned that I was working with people who lacked integrity, that they had a bad reputation for taking the money and not doing the work, at least not well, and for taking advantage of the system. He thought that my associating with them would be harmful to my career. He suggested I write a book about the companies I worked for and experiences I had with clients, but that didn't resonate with me. I wanted something else. I just wasn't sure what.

I got to thinking about the quality of care Julie had provided me and what set her apart from the rest. I imagined how it would have felt, when I first went to Julie, to have her not care, to not feel with me, to not connect, to not actually help me. That was what I had experienced at home with my family. No one had helped me. I had had to keep myself together. I had had to raise myself. And because I had lacked what I needed as a child, my foundation was unstable. I had needed a new one, and I had built myself with Julie's help. If someone had gone through the motions with me, pretending help, promising it when I so desperately needed it and then not actually giving it, I am not sure how I would have survived. Julie had truly cared about me, and she had given her utmost, and that had made all the difference. With her, I felt safe enough to let the pieces of myself come apart, and then to put them back together. I wanted to be there for others the way she had been for me. I had always wished that someone had helped me sooner, so I decided that I would study in order to learn how to help children in need.

It took me slightly more than two years to get my master's degree at Pepperdine. I was the first person on either side of my family to get an advanced degree. My parents were both very proud of my achievement, but my dad was thrilled. The day of my graduation he couldn't stop beaming. He kept taking pictures and saying that this was so exciting.

After the ceremony he took us to the Sand Castle, a very expensive, exclusive little restaurant known mostly to the locals in Malibu. My nephew was four at the time, and after we had lunch, we all went out on the beach and he ran around and played in the surf while we walked along. It was such a lovely day.

It was much later that I realized that the happiness my dad felt that day had everything to do with my achievement. He couldn't just be happy. I had to have *done* something. I couldn't just *be* someone.

While earning my master's degree, I met someone who was taking a summer vacation to study another language in another country. The program was called Language Studies Abroad.

Many people where I live speak Spanish and very little English. I decided it would help me do my job better if I could speak some of their language, so I signed up. After a two-week immersion program in Costa Rica, I knew that I wanted to continue.

I found a Spanish teacher in the LA area who taught weekend classes to working adults. Cecilia was from Chile. She called to assess my level and put me in an intermediate class. When I finished that one, I continued studying with her. Then she told me that she had a private advanced conversation class that she taught in her home salon.

Cecilia suggested two books. They were like dictionaries with Spanish words and phrases in them. At that time, my parents were trying hard to be supportive. When I told them about the new class and the books, my mom went out and bought them for me.

My parents were very proud of what I was doing. My mother was also glad that I was going back to church. I didn't talk much about going to 12 Step meetings. My mother knew I was going, and at one point, she went for quite a while and said they helped her a lot, but she eventually stopped going; I'm not sure why. Still, she thanked me for telling her about them. She hadn't known they existed.

I began using my Spanish with clients. I did immersion programs in Mexico, Ecuador, and Guatemala and studied with Cecilia when I could. I'm still in touch with her today.

I found my passion working for the Los Angeles County Department of Children and Family Services and for some small private agencies doing social work or child therapy, and I did this work for the next 20 years. Using my life experience, my empathy, I was determined to help as many children and families as I could break the cycle. I felt empathy for the parents too, because at this point, I could finally look at my parents and see why they were as they were—flawed, but worthy of compassion and love. Yes, they had hurt me, but love doesn't just disappear because someone hurts you. And now I could take that hurt and use it to help.

Another good thing fell into place when they asked me to sing in the choir at my church. I had also started fostering animals from rescue shelters. These animals had been abused, neglected, and abandoned by their previous owners. They were to be euthanized because they were homeless and no one wanted them. Fostering them brought such sweetness into my life.

One day, I turned around and realized that I had a life that I really enjoyed. I was a lot happier. I was healing. I knew if I had a bad day at work, or stuff was going on in my family, I could open up the book and find an Al Anon meeting. I could go and talk, or I could just listen to other people sharing their stories. I wasn't alone.

The strands of my life had frayed, but I had taken those strands and some new ones and made myself a new life. A life I loved.

In 2003, I decided that it was time to get a PhD while continuing to work full time.

Pepperdine graduation day receiving my Master's Degree. A beautiful day in May at Malibu Beach on the Pacific Ocean.

Me wearing my Venice Boardwalk cat glasses. Looking very happy!

Family reunion Maga's 90th birthday uncle's 60th birthday parents' 40th wedding anniversary Ohio River paddleboat cruise

THERAPY

My Nephew

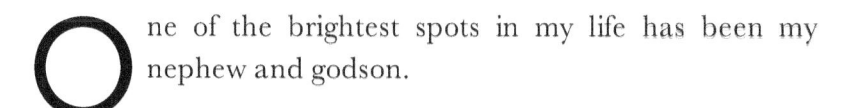

One of the brightest spots in my life has been my nephew and godson.

From the very start, we were very close. I loved spending time with him. He brought a warmth and joy to my life that I hadn't had with other members of my family. I took him to Disneyland, Barnum and Bailey Circus, and Cirque du Soleil, and I celebrated milestones with him. When he got into sports, I would watch him play soccer, baseball, and basketball and take him out after his games.

He was very good at sports, and his parents pushed him to excel. When he was 12, he started having panic attacks and trouble sleeping, so my sister took him to a child psychologist who determined that my sister and her husband had pushed their child to the point where he couldn't handle the pressure. He was expected to beat everyone, to be better than everyone at everything. It was like nothing else mattered, including him: he was not innately valuable. I think of it as not being treated like a human "being," but as a human "doing." This was how my father was, as well. Achievement was everything.

My sister and her husband weren't involved in activities. They were living vicariously through him, and they were crushing him. They were in total control. One summer, his dad said he was going to sign my nephew up for baseball camp so he could be a better player. My nephew said he didn't want that, so his father told him that he'd work on scout badges. He wasn't asked. He was told. He had no control over his own life.

As he got older, I saw him less often. He was a teenager. Aunts aren't as much fun when you're a teenager. But I heard through my parents that he was doing better. My mother told me that the child psychologist was helping him learn to assert himself with his parents. He improved, but he just wasn't strong enough to fight them.

He made it through high school with good grades and went to a college a few hours from home. I was so glad he got in to a school far from them. They couldn't control him the same way.

When he came home that first Christmas, it was obvious there was something wrong. He didn't smile. He didn't seem himself at all.

In March, my mom called to say that my nephew had been diagnosed with OCD. He had been behaving strangely at school, which made it hard for him to make friends. This had never been an issue with him before. Even his grades had been suffering, despite the fact that he was a very bright young man.

They got him on medication, and things improved. It made me think of what I had gone through during my first year away from home, and I hoped that he would find the same kind of healing that I had at university.

I started visiting him twice a year and watched him picking his own sport and his own major. He was finally able to make his own decisions.

He made good friends. I talked to him about not going home when he graduated. He had roommates, and they invited him to stay, but when I took him out to celebrate his graduation, he said he was moving home for a while.

I must have looked worried, because he said, "Don't worry, Aunt Shauna, it'll just be for a little while."

I hid my dismay the best I could. I knew once he moved back in with them, he wouldn't get out. They needed him there. They had no accomplishments of their own. He was their accomplishment. They had no identity. He was their identity. But there was nothing I could do. Home he went. He found a good job, one he enjoyed, but he lived in their house on their terms.

Meanwhile, I was dealing with my own crisis.

Dr. Jack

The thing about being raised in an unhealthy family is that you don't have a solid foundation. You can work at building up a foundation for yourself, but you're always building on top of that unstable one you were given by the lack you experienced in your early years. I had built up a stronger foundation with Julie, but anything cobbled together crumbles at some point. That's what finally happened in 2009. Out of the blue, I began having panic attacks. At least, it seemed like they were out of the blue.

At first I had panic attacks during the day. Then I started waking up with horrifying nightmares, in a cold sweat with my heart racing. I had thought I was doing well. I lived in a nice apartment in a nice area. I had a good job. I was healthy. My relationships with my family seemed better. I had my animals. Life was good. So what was happening to me?

I told my friend Keith, who had known me for many years and was a dear, wise friend. He told me to go talk to someone.

I looked up doctors I could see on my plan. There was only one nearby.

I'll call him Dr. Jack.

When I phoned Dr. Jack that day, he asked me what was going on. He wanted to see if there was something he could help me with.

He listened to me describe the panic attacks. He said, "OK, makes it sounds like you really need to see somebody. I'm going to fit you into my schedule. Today."

I'll never forget that first session. Dr. Jack listened, and then he laid out what was happening. A, B, and C. And he just nailed it. I couldn't believe he could listen to me for a few minutes and understand me so well. He told me that he had been doing this work for 45 years. He was 72 at the time and not retiring any time soon because he loved what he did.

He prescribed medication for the depression he diagnosed me with, and for the anxiety, but he said meds were a Band-Aid solution. He wanted to help me figure out what was going on underneath all that.

And so, once again, I was learning to express myself and assert myself, to stop bottling things up. I was 50 at the time. He told me he couldn't believe I had hung on for as long as I had. He said he was going to help me learn not to hold everything inside so I didn't get stuck like this again. He told me to have fun, to not work all the time. To just enjoy myself.

He looked at me and said, "We're going get to know each other really well, Shauna."

And we did. I ended up seeing Dr. Jack for the next 11 years. I really needed him for what was to come.

A Sweet Blast From My Past

UCLA has excellent research libraries, which I used when I began work on my dissertation. I picked a topic that one of my professors thought might help me to get a job when I got out. It had to do with child custody and children of divorce.

I started seeing a certain name on a lot of the articles I was reading. The work was published by a woman living in the San Francisco Bay Area. Her first name was Julie. I didn't recognize her surname, but I remembered that my therapist all those years ago at UCLA had moved to San Francisco because of her boyfriend, and then I remembered that this had been the field that she was interested in. All the pieces came together. I had found my Julie.

I hadn't been in touch with her since I'd graduated from UCLA. I had sent her an announcement of my graduation to let her know that I had done it, and she wrote me the loveliest letter of congratulations and said she liked to think she had played a small part in my achievement. I replied to say that she had played a *huge* part.

I had always wanted Julie to know how much I appreciated what she had done for me, to tell her how I was and what I was doing with my life. I did that now. I contacted the woman who had co-authored many of the articles, and she connected me with Julie.

I wrote to tell her how wonderful she was, that I'd never forgotten her, that she helped me get through school and that horrible time. She had helped me understand what happened to me when I was growing up and set me on a path to healing. I told her that she would always be an extremely important person in my life. I told her about my master's degree and that I was now getting a PhD.

I realized that many years had gone by, and many people would have passed through her life, but when she wrote back, she said she had very fond memories of me.

In one article she published, she wrote that she had always wanted to do research and teach rather than be a clinician, and this is what she had been doing all these years at San Francisco State. I was surprised, because she had helped me so much. She really had been excellent at it. I was grateful that she was required to do that clinical internship to get her license; otherwise, I would never have had her as a therapist. I learned that on the day my case was read out, she had thought it sounded interesting and raised her hand to take it. I'll always be grateful for that.

We wrote for a time, but it trickled off. I think it bothered me that the powerful bond that was formed during psychodynamic therapy at UCLA was now a distant one.

My 35th birthday celebration with my family. My nephew Karsten helped me celebrate with my cake. My Mom baked the cake.

My nephew's kindergarten school photo. Whittier California. He was 5 years old. So adorable!

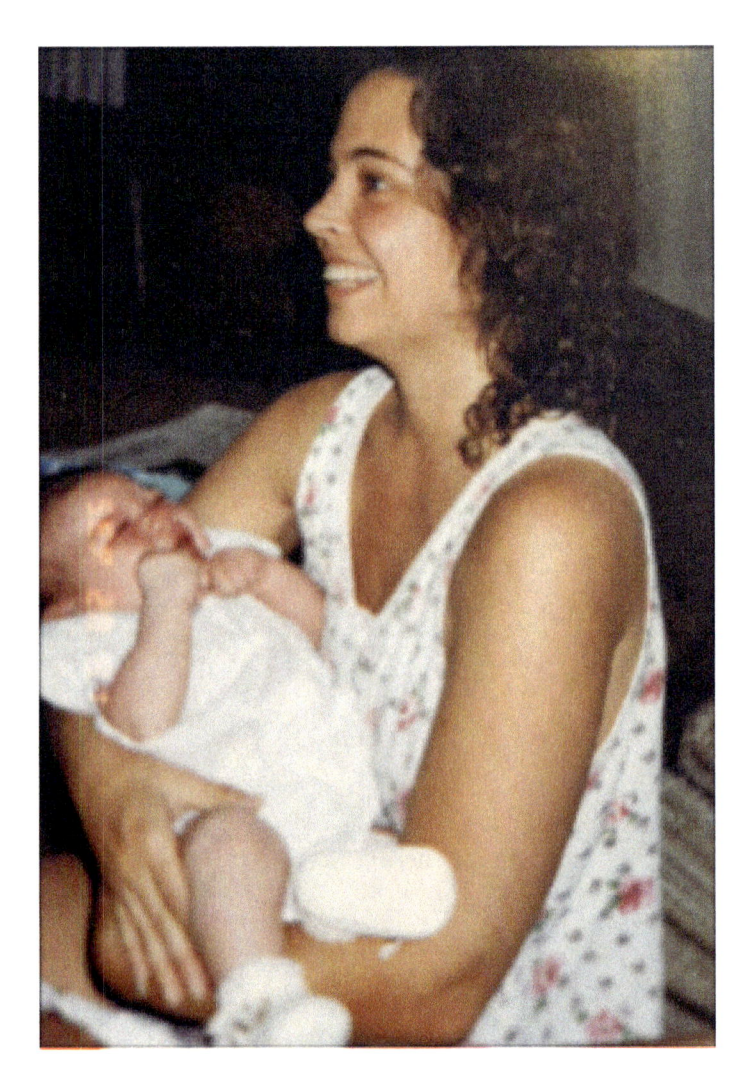

Me holding my nephew and godson right after his birth. I was so thrilled to be an aunt.

My nephew Karsten's graduation from Cal Poly San Luis Obispo. A beautiful day in June at SLO. Another very happy day!

June 26, 1938 - February 25, 2021

*Dr Jack my wonderful therapist helped me with so many difficult times in my life
Miss him so much Rest in Eternal Peace*

THE END OF MY FAMILY

It was a hard road, but I finally got my PhD. I credit Dr. Jack with getting me through it.

My graduation was a really big deal. Friends, relatives, people from church, and even people who knew my parents sent me congratulations and cards. Some even sent money. People attended the graduation with balloons and flowers and gifts and cards for their graduating loved ones. My parents were so proud and made a huge deal of the event, but my sister and her family showed up late and empty-handed and sat glumly throughout the proceedings. They didn't clap when I crossed the stage and seemed to resent having to be there. My nephew wasn't much better. I think he was very happy for me, but he showed up without a card or a gift. I remember feeling a little hurt because of how much I'd always done for him. It should have been a great day for me. Instead I felt sad and let down. I knew my sister and her husband were incapable of being happy for me, but there was something spiteful in their need to ruin my celebration, as if stealing some of my joy would make them feel better about themselves.

Dr. Jack helped me see that this was their narcissism, which is a *what's in it for me?* attitude to life. There was nothing in it for them to cheer me on. In fact, I had won a bigger trophy than either of them. They couldn't like that.

IT BEGINS WITH ME

I defended my dissertation on December 7th, 2010 and went back to working full time.

A year later, just before Thanksgiving, my dad called to ask me if I could come over to help get my mother into bed. He said she had collapsed, and he thought maybe she needed to be in the hospital, but he was vague. He had been diagnosed with mild dementia, so sometimes he got things confused. I thought this was one of those times. I was an hour away, and I had plans that day, and because he didn't sound particularly alarmed, I asked if it could wait a bit. I was going to be in that area that afternoon. I would come over later.

He agreed, so I went to my event, and in the early evening, I arrived at my parents' house. It was completely dark. I found my dad sitting in the darkened TV room. I asked him where mom, was and he said she was in the bedroom lying down.

When I saw my mom, I had the fright of my life. She looked pale and lifeless, like she was already gone. If my father had described this to me, I would have come right away!

He had called 911 earlier, but she had refused to go with the paramedics. They had suggested he call his children and see if they could convince her to go to the hospital, because she really needed medical attention.

I told her how worried I was and that I wanted to get her to the hospital. She agreed, but only if there were no sirens. I had a better idea. The hospital was five minutes away. I got her to lie down in the back seat of my car and took her in. At the ER, she couldn't walk in the door. They immediately got her into a wheelchair and onto oxygen, which seemed to bring her back to life.

IT BEGINS WITH ME

She had suffered congestive heart failure.

She stayed in the hospital for a few days. The doctors told us that she would always have to have oxygen. They taught me to check her oxygen and explained all the other things someone would have to do for her. She would never be able to take care of herself again.

I worked full time and lived almost an hour away. There was no way my dad could handle all of this, and my sister didn't want to help. He had called her that day too. She lived only 20 minutes away, but she hadn't come. I had to find someone to help. I made calls to set up the services my parents needed. My mom needed occupational therapy and nurses to help with her oxygen and medications and other care. My dad couldn't remember these things. I got in a home healthcare provider, because she needed to be on a special heart diet. Someone would come in to prepare meals and clean up and do other basic things around the house. It was a lot of work, but finally there were good supports in place.

My mom started doing better. She could get around with a walker and seemed more herself. My dad and I worked together as a team for the next few weeks, but that Christmas, my sister and her husband learned at the dinner table that my parents and I had set up in-home healthcare, and they were very displeased. They felt it was costing too much money, despite the fact that this was my parents' money, and they were in a very good financial position at that point in their lives. My parents had set up a trust. Half would go to my sister and half to me after our parents were gone. I believe my sister and her husband were worried how these costs were chipping away at their inheritance.

My parents had also split power of attorney down the middle, giving my sister control over financial matters and putting me in charge of medical decisions. My sister tried to cut off the in-home care by refusing to pay for it until my parents' attorney who had set up the trust and the powers of attorney for them informed her that medical decisions supersede financial ones. She and her husband continued to argue that we were spending too much money, but they had no choice in the matter.

That didn't stop them from complaining about every decision I made. Phone calls, emails, and complaints to my parents filtered back to me, all with the message that I was spending too much. When I told them they could take over, they didn't want that. They didn't want to help at all. They wanted me to do the work, but they wanted to control what I did and complain when I didn't do what they wanted. We had a lot of ugly conversations about money and how this was our parents' money and they had earned it and now they needed it. It was very upsetting, even more so because I knew my mother's time with us was limited.

And I was right. She lived five months. But before she died, something happened that was perhaps the ugliest thing my sister has ever done. She secretly canceled the home care. I only found out after the company called to ask if I knew about this. I did not. No one had said a thing. Not even my parents. They had kept silent for at least a month while they struggled alone.

I got support back into my parents' home, but my mom hadn't received proper care for all those weeks, and her health had deteriorated. She was hospitalized in February for a short time, and then again in March. This time the doctor told me he thought it was time to recommend hospice.

I think my grieving began at that point. I cried when I told Dr. Jack what was happening, because I just knew my mother was going to be gone soon. I felt so hurt on so many levels, and so alone. He talked me through it, and I found my footing, knowing I had him there to lean on.

I found an excellent in-home hospice. I visited my mom every weekend, staying with my dad so I could help him at home.

Then one day in April I was on my way to visit my mom when my sister called to tell me that I should get there fast.

"Shauna," she said, "Mom turned blue."

I wish I could say that my mother's death brought us all closer. It didn't. My sister and I did briefly come together to comfort her in those final hours, to read to her from the Bible and hold her hands and tell her we loved her. I gave her permission to go. I told her that I would be all right. In the low moments that came later, the promise I made to her would be a blessing to me.

But my father could not face the reality of losing her and kept insisting she would rally, so he didn't say goodbye to her or tell her that he loved her. I know he did love her, but all he could think about while she was dying was his own loss. My mother died with her two daughters holding her hands, and her husband denying that she was leaving him.

I believe that the only reason she lived those five months after her first heart failure was to give all of us time to accept the inevitable, but especially him. And it wasn't enough.

My mother donated her body to science because of her scoliosis and other medical issues, so we had to wait for hours for them to come for her body. And then she really was gone. We were in my parents' house—now my dad's house—and the others wanted to eat. I couldn't even think of eating, so I left them there, sitting around the table eating like we hadn't just lost Mom.

Little did I know, that would be the last time I would be in that house for a very long time.

A few days later, my uncle called to tell me that the locks had been changed on the house. He told me I wasn't welcome there anymore. Nor was I welcome to speak at my mother's funeral. The whole thing was planned without me and excluding me. I went and spoke anyway.

And then I learned that my sister had in fact been very busy while I was caring for our parents. She had gotten power of attorney for Dad's medical decisions and had convinced him to change financial advisers in 2009. The new advisor was a friend of theirs.

I called my dad. He spoke to me as if I were his enemy. He didn't want to see me or talk to me. They had convinced him that I was a bad person. I realized that he had been different with me ever since the home care people had been fired. I think they'd been working on him for a while. I kept trying to talk with my dad, to see him, but he continued to reject me.

Dr. Jack and my friends agreed that I should stop calling, stop begging. My sister and her husband were playing a vicious game with me. So that summer I grieved alone and with the support of Dr. Jack, friends, and people in my Al Anon community. My nephew reached out to me now and then, but I wasn't invited to Thanksgiving or Christmas that year. At some point I realized that I wasn't part of the family anymore.

I took some time off work. I kept on with meetings and church and seeing Dr. Jack, but I was hurting.

One day I saw something online about animals being euthanized in shelters and how people were trying to rescue them. This really upset me. When I was a girl, there were times that I felt the only unconditional love I got was from the animals we had, especially the dogs. I started donating money. I had three cats at that point, but I thought I could foster a small dog.

Rocky was my first foster. He was an adorable old black-and-white Applehead Chihuahua. He was with me for a year before he crossed over the Rainbow Bridge.

I kept fostering and even did some adopting. The two dogs I have to this day were fosters that I fell so in love with that I had to keep them.

Giving love to these animals that had never known any love, and getting love back from them, helped, but I still felt like I was falling apart again. I missed my mom. I felt orphaned. I couldn't process what had happened to my family. I didn't know how I was ever going to feel healthy and whole.

One day, about six months after my mother died, Dr. Jack told me his story.

He was born to Jewish parents in Poland in 1938 and was a young boy when his father saw the writing on the wall and got them out to France where they stayed out in the country, moving from place to place to avoid people discovering that they were Jews. They found food where they could, sometimes in dumpsters.

The war ended, and they eventually decided that they wanted out of Europe, so they took passage on a boat to the United States.

Dr. Jack got tears in his eyes when he told me about being eleven years old and seeing the Statue of Liberty as they arrived in the U.S.A. He described how he had to learn English and was struggling and how one of his teachers reached out to help him and how much that meant to him. He decided that he wanted to do the same for other people. He trained to be a doctor with a specialty in anesthesiology.

Vietnam was still going on when he graduated. He wanted to give back to the United States for giving his family a safe haven, so he volunteered for the Air Force. He did two tours of duty there, using his training in anesthesiology. Sometimes he served as a General Practitioner. He was well past the age of the draft at that point. He volunteered to serve others, because that's the kind of person that he was.

He explained why he was telling me all this. He said that once he realized that what had happened to him in Europe was the worst thing that could ever happen to him, he knew he could get through anything. He said that losing my mom, and my family turning their backs on me, was one of the worst things that would ever happen to me, but that I could get through it, just as I'd gotten through my childhood. He had taken his awful experiences and turned them into something positive. People had helped him, so he dedicated his life to helping others. He survived and thrived. So would I.

I knew he was right. I also knew that he had faith in me. I put my energy into helping others and moving on with my life.

One year after my mom died, a year of almost no contact with my family, my dad called to tell me that he was in the hospital. He'd had congestive heart failure.

I made the mistake of saying I'd come to visit him. My sister and her husband were there when I arrived. They wanted me to take over all the responsibility for Dad's care, but they would continue to hold the purse strings and make the decisions. I would just do the work. I thought about it. My dad had allowed them to take control. They had cut me out of the family.

I told them to do it all themselves. They were furious.

I had limited contact with my dad after that. He did call me sometimes. He sent me a card and gift at Christmas, and then at my birthday. He called during a heatwave to ask how my animals and I were holding up, did we have air conditioning, that sort of thing. When I did see him, he always seemed happy to see me. I sometimes spoke to the caregiver who helped him at home before he finally had to go into assisted living, and she said he missed me.

The next time he went into the hospital—he had some falls because he refused to use a walker—we had a good visit. As I was leaving, I told him I loved him. He had oxygen on his face. He pulled the mask off and said, "I love you, too."

I went back the next day, and this time, when I left, he beat me to the punch. He told me he loved me. I told him I loved him very much.

I believe that he felt safe saying this to me because my sister and her husband weren't around. Later, this was confirmed for me by the caregiver, who witnessed much of what went on in my family during that first year that I was excluded from it.

Unfortunately, the last time I saw my dad, on his birthday, he was hostile towards me. He told me he didn't want to see me. Ten days later, when I called to ask how he had liked my gift, he thanked me. I sensed he felt guilty.

At 6:30 p.m. on October 28, 2015, my nephew called to tell me that my dad had died early that morning, about 12 hours before, alone in his room after a fall.

My nephew called almost every day after that, sometimes more than once a day. He called to invite me to the funeral and to tell me that I could bring whomever I wanted.

The funeral took place a few weeks later. My dad had arranged to be buried in the VA cemetery at Riverside, and my mom's ashes would be buried with him. This went expressly against her wishes, which were to be buried with her family in Ohio. I think my sister and her husband didn't want to spend the money to do that. I also think that my dad worried that they would go against his wishes, so he made his own arrangements. In that way, I suppose he finally took care of himself.

IT BEGINS WITH ME

This time, they realized I was going to speak no matter what, so they allowed it. I spoke for my aunt and uncle, who hadn't been able to make it, and then I spoke for myself.

The funeral was very hard for me. They played Taps and read a poem by Alfred Lord Tennyson called "Crossing the Bar" about moving past a sandbar to venture into the ocean. It was a metaphor for death. He had arranged to have that poem read and printed on little cards to be given to those in attendance. He had always been at peace on the water.

I got through the holidays alone, and then in January, I learned that what I feared had happened. Not only had my dad given my sister power of attorney when he was alive, but he had disinherited me a few days before he moved into assisted living. To make matters even worse, my sister tried to go after the share of the Trust my mom had set up for us. She wanted her half and mine. She tried to claim that I had been given money to get my PhD, a degree that I wasn't even using. Neither thing was true. Fortunately, it was an irrevocable trust. My sister was successful regarding some parts of the war she fought against me, but not on that one. I did receive the money that my mom left for me from her share of the Trust.

My mother would have been horrified at what they did, and furious at my father for allowing them to pressure him. I think she saw it coming. Before she died, she made him promise not to change the Trust. He kept that promise for two years. He wasn't a strong man. He eventually gave in.

Now we really went to war. They said I was a terrible daughter and my father hadn't wanted me near him. I endured character assassination and a mind-boggling twisting of facts. It was devastatingly ugly, and it cost me a lot of money to fight them, but I needed to do it, if only to show them that I knew what they had done. To push back. To stand up for myself.

They were furious about how much it cost them to fight me, because during that time, my nephew stopped speaking to me. It was obvious that they told him to stop talking to me after I received the share of the Trust that my mom left for me.

The one bright spot was that my father's caregiver agreed to a deposition, which is how I learned the truth about so many things.

The caregiver was present when my sister and her husband showed up with a financial adviser and tried to force my dad to sign some papers. He got very upset and refused. They fed him alcohol despite the fact that he was not supposed to mix alcohol with his medications. They didn't want to pay for a caregiver on Saturday and Sunday, so he went to their house on weekends. He told the caregiver how poorly they treated him.

She told us that my father had held a card I sent him to his heart and kissed it and that he had cried. She said that he had been miserable about not seeing me, that he said he missed me. She described how happy he was at times when I called. She said that my sister would go through his phone to see who he had called and give him a hard time if she saw my number in it. He would tell my sister he wanted to talk to me, to see me, and she'd tell him he didn't need to be talking to me, that she didn't want to see my number in his phone anymore. He would put my sister on speaker phone so the caregiver could hear the way my sister talked to him. My sister was mean and cold and commanding.

She said all this and much more in a very long deposition.

My attorney told me that as the caregiver told her story, my sister's breathing grew harder, as if she were having a panic attack, or she was in a rage.

It was heartbreaking for me to learn that my father had been abused in this way, but it helped me too. It paved the way for healing to know that my father had loved me. He had wanted me in his life.

The caregiver promised to testify in court, but that didn't happen. She was so defiant, so eager to speak, and she told me she was more than willing to come back, but something happened to change that. I learned that their attorney had called her. I complained to the bar that my witness had been threatened, and they backed off, but she wouldn't come back. Unfortunately, she was living in another state and was out of subpoena range.

I spent three awful years fighting them, but in the end, they won my father's share of the Trust.

The caregiver let me down, but I can't hold that against her. She gave me what I needed. People thought my fight was about the money. It wasn't. It was about how he cut me out of his will and why. I couldn't just accept that. I didn't believe he would do that to me voluntarily, and this woman helped me to know that I was right about that. About my dad. Flawed as he was, he loved me.

Dr. Jack and my friends gave me the rest of what I needed. They told me not to become bitter, to move on, to let karma do its thing. They told me the best revenge was living well.

It was hard, but I knew they all spoke out of love and concern for me. They wanted what was best for me. Besides, I had made a promise to my mother when she died that I would be all right. I had to keep that promise.

And I have. I have learned how to be all right.

Part of that process has included telling my story. Telling the truth instead of burying it. Letting it out instead of bottling it up inside.

My Dad took me to lunch at Cheesecake Factory in Marina del Rey where I lived at the time after my Mom died. Nice time!

My parents' grave at the VA Cemetery Riverside. I scattered rose petals on Mother's Day. Rose is Mom's favorite flower.

My Mom hugging her beloved only grandson. Sweet picture.

Dad's retirement party from Converse Consultants after 31 years as a geologist. We all came to it. Monrovia, California

Mom, Dad, and I saw Christo the artist yellow umbrella art display, Gorman, California. Mom and Dad hugging an umbrella.

WHERE I'M AT AND WHERE I'M GOING

These days, I'm more than all right.

It took time and hard work to move forward, but I kept doing all the things that I do—church and Al Anon and therapy, friends and work and fostering animals, walking on the beach, being grateful for my many blessings—and I left much of the hurt behind me.

Then the pandemic happened. So many people struggled financially during COVID, but my PhD served me well. A recruiter got me working with the homeless in L.A. during the week, and on weekends, I worked with foster kids. More recently, I have been working in the state of Washington in men's prisons. My life is busy and rich and full.

In January 2021, Dr. Jack called to tell me that he was going to be retiring. I was devastated. I was doing so much better, but I felt that I needed him. I told him that I wanted to see him one more time to say goodbye.

In that last session, he told me I was going to be fine. He said I should call him in June. He made it sound like he was just taking some time off, not going away for good.

When I called after the 4th of July, I learned that he had died on February 25th, five weeks after the last time I saw him.

I had communicated with one of his daughters in the past, and she gave me more details. He had been diagnosed with a very unusual, aggressive type of Leukemia, but he hadn't expected it to go that fast. He had fully expected to be there when I called.

She told me that she had heard a lot about me and that her father thought the world of me, that he had cared deeply for me, that he had believed in me, that he had known I would be fine.

What a brilliant, loving, generous man he was. How grateful I will always be to him for seeing my inner strength and teaching me how to dig down into it, to grab hold of it and believe in it, to believe in myself. He gave me the tools to endure whatever pain or grief might come, and to move beyond it.

When he told me I'd be fine, he was right, as usual. I will always miss him, but I'll be fine.

***

I wrote this book at this point in my life in the hopes that sharing my experiences will help others. If just one person seeks help and experiences some healing as a result of reading my story, it will be worth it. Getting everything out, exposing the secrets once again, has also provided me with more healing.

And now I'm planning my next phase. I'll work some more in the field I'm in, perhaps taking jobs in different places to see them, to experience more of the world. I will keep going with all the activities that enrich my life and provide the connections that sustain me. I want to do more for animals and see more of the world.

Whatever happens, I have hope that it will be good. I have hope! That's something I never thought I would say when I was a forlorn, frightened, powerless girl all those years ago.

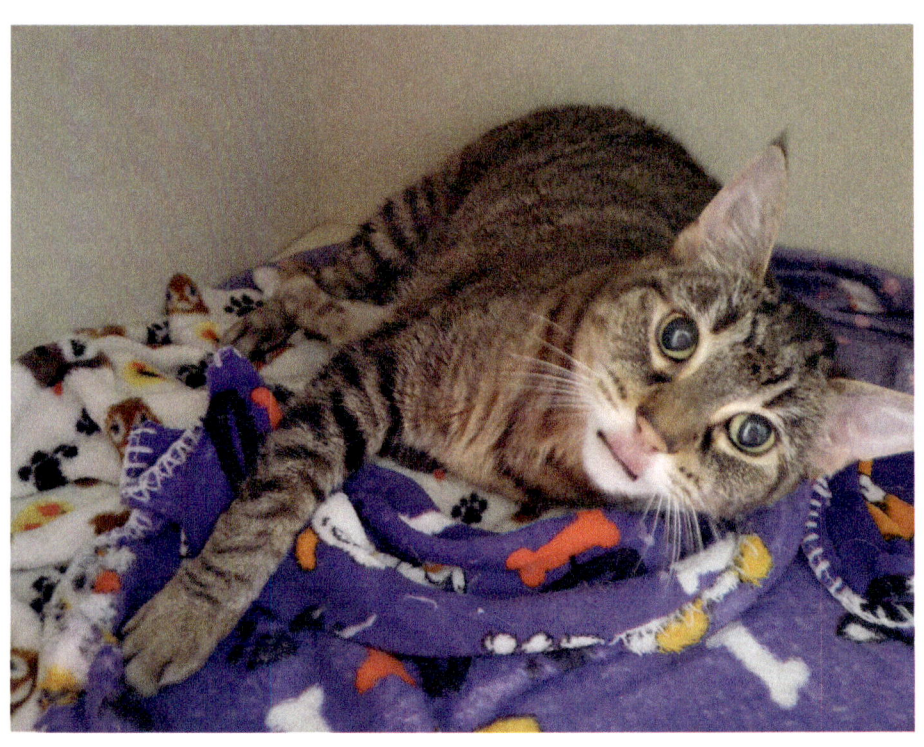

Cheyenne one of three littermates adopted from a shelter Tintypes looked exactly alike. My little angel still with me 🐾🐾

Merry Corgi mix rescue I adopted Country Kennels doggy water park in Riverside. What a bathing beauty!

Dylan sweet chihuahua mix rescue I adopted completely blind Race for the Rescues Dog Walk Rose Bowl Pasadena California

WHAT I WANT YOU TO KNOW

There are some things I want you to know.

No matter what has happened to you, you can not only survive it, you can thrive.
It took me a long time to believe this. In the end, I had to prove it to myself. Choose to believe it. Act on it. You'll make it come true.

There's no shame in needing help. There's no shame in asking for help.
I'm not sure where we humans get the idea that we should be able to do everything on our own, but we seem to cling to it like it's a higher truth. It's not. You show strength when you reach for help. You show courage and strength. You have these things inside you already, but you may need help to harness them so they can serve you better.

People want to help you.
The people who came into my life when I needed them were there because I reached for them. But they gave of themselves because they wanted to. Sylvia, Julie, Dr. Jack, my friends at school, so many friends after them, and so many strangers who were learning to heal and wanted to share that

healing with me. Yes, I reached out, but they chose to give. They were and are my angels.

It's not wrong to tell your story.

Even after all these years, I still feel that I am being disloyal to my family, and especially to my dad, by talking about what happened in our family. I wish I could say there's a way to heal without sharing our stories with others. I don't believe there is. If you keep the truth inside, you are denying your own wounds. They will fester.

If you struggle with this feeling of disloyalty, there is a solution: tell your story with love. By talking about what happened in my family, I came to understand my mother and father as human beings, deeply flawed because he was deeply wounded and didn't know how to heal himself. I can't help but feel compassion for him when I see him that way. If I'd kept the truth inside, I am not sure I would have come to see them this way.

I hope it's clear that I loved my family very much, even at the worst times. I hope that my parents would bless what I've done by telling this story. But the fact remains that at the end of the day, this is my story, not theirs. It's mine to heal through the telling of it.

Telling your story can help others heal.

Hearing other people tell their stories in Al Anon meetings helped me enormously. It made me feel that others understood what I went through and was going through. It made me feel less alone. It also showed me that it was OK to talk about all of it. They were already exposing the secret we all shared, and the sky wasn't falling on them.

In the past, I've shared my story in order to heal myself, but I'm telling it here in order to help others with their healing. People attending meetings or getting therapy are already on the path to healing. My hope is that this book will reach those who aren't talking yet, so they can begin healing too.

It can begin with you too.

I wish someone in my family had chosen to heal before I came along, but no one did. I had to be the one to get the ball rolling. I chose to break the pattern, to pass on healing instead of pain. The children I have helped through my work are my kids. I recognized what I needed when I was a girl and gave as much of that as I could to them. I hope that I planted a seed of healing in all of them and that they made the choice to heal.

I hope that someday my nephew will do the same, that he will break free and become his own person and know just how much he is worth. Enormous accomplishments or none.

In the meantime, I continue to use what I have learned to help others. I will only make this journey of life once. If there is something that I can do to help someone else while I am here, I will do it. I want to make it a journey of purpose, to give back what I've been given. This, to me, is the ultimate victory. The healing begins with me, but it doesn't end with me.

It doesn't need to end with you either. You too can heal and change your life for the better.

Me smiling and happy after all my hard work using self help and professional help to heal. Living a good life!

StoryTerrace

Printed in Great Britain
by Amazon